Contents

All about media

What do ads, **blogs** and news reports have in common? They are types of media. Books, websites, films, TV programmes and **apps** are media as well. Media sends a message. An **audience** receives the message.

FACT⬛⬛⬛⬛⬛⬛⬛NS:

T⬛

AD⬛

BRIEN J JENNINGS

Raintree is an imprint of Capstone Global Library Limited, a company incorporated in England and Wales having its registered office at 264 Banbury Road, Oxford, OX2 7DY – Registered company number: 6695582

www.raintree.co.uk
myorders@raintree.co.uk

Printed and bound in India

ISBN 978 1 4747 5441 5 (hardback)
22 21 20 19 18
10 9 8 7 6 5 4 3 2 1

ISBN 978 1 4747 5445 3 (paperback)
23 22 21 20 19
10 9 8 7 6 5 4 3 2 1

Editorial credits:
Erika L. Shores, editor; Juliette ████ ████ designer;
Morgan Walters, media researc████ Kathy McColley, production specialist

Photo credits:
Alamy: Agencja Fotograficzna C████ █████ Greenberg 6 of 6, 17; ████ ███terstock: Africa Studio, 11, Akkaradet Bangchu██ ████ ██ ████ Vasyukova, 20, Asier_B (icons) design ████ement, Charts and Table, Cover, Denis Rozhnovsk███ ████ ███ ████ ████ng) 12, Duplass, left Cover███ Mat Hayward, 7, MITstudio, (drink) 12, MK pho███ ██████ ██ ████ ██ ██ Roman Tiraspolsky, 13, ███pphachai Salaeman, design element throughout, VG █████ ██ ████ ███ ██████ ████ ████ ███brea████ ███edia, 9

**British Library Cataloguing██ ██ ████████ ████
A full catalogue record for t██ ████ ██ ██████████ ████ ██ ███ British Library.

Every effort has been made ██ ███████ copyright holde███ ██ ████████ ██████████ ██ this book. Any omissions will be rectified in subsequent printings if notice is given to the publisher.

blog diary on the internet; blog is short for weblog
app programme that is downloaded to computers and
    mobile devices; app is short for application
audience people who hear, read or see a message

5

Who is the audience for media messages? You are! So it's up to you to ask a lot of questions. Ask questions to understand the media maker's **purpose**. Why was the message created? Understanding the purpose helps you to work out if the media's message is fact, fiction or opinion.

purpose reason for which something is made or done

Media informs, entertains and **persuades**. Media that informs includes facts. Facts are true. We check facts by finding **evidence**.

If the purpose of media is to entertain, then it may be fiction. Fiction is not true. It is made up.

Sometimes the purpose of media is to persuade. This type of media often includes opinions. An opinion is an idea or feeling about something. An opinion is not the same as a fact. We can't prove opinions are true.

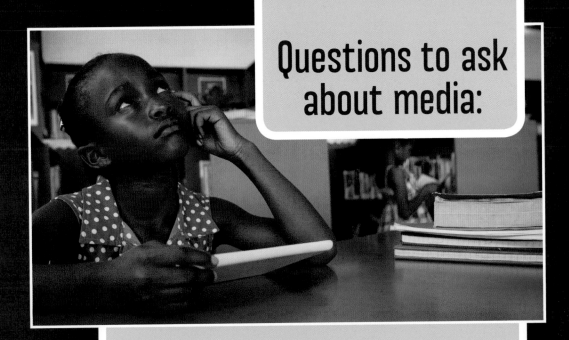

Questions to ask about media:

Who created the media?

Who is the audience for the media?

How does the author try to keep the audience's attention?

Why was the media created?

Does it give important information (inform)?

Does it tell a story, make you laugh, cry or feel a certain way (entertain)?

Does it try to change your mind or convince you of something (persuade)?

evidence information, items and facts that help prove something to be true or false

persuade change a person's mind

Ads

Advertisements, also called ads, are made to sell something. They're not fiction, and they're not always an opinion. The main purpose of an ad is to persuade or to get you to buy something. Ads may also try to change your mind about a topic or product.

---

advertisement notice that calls attention to a product or an event

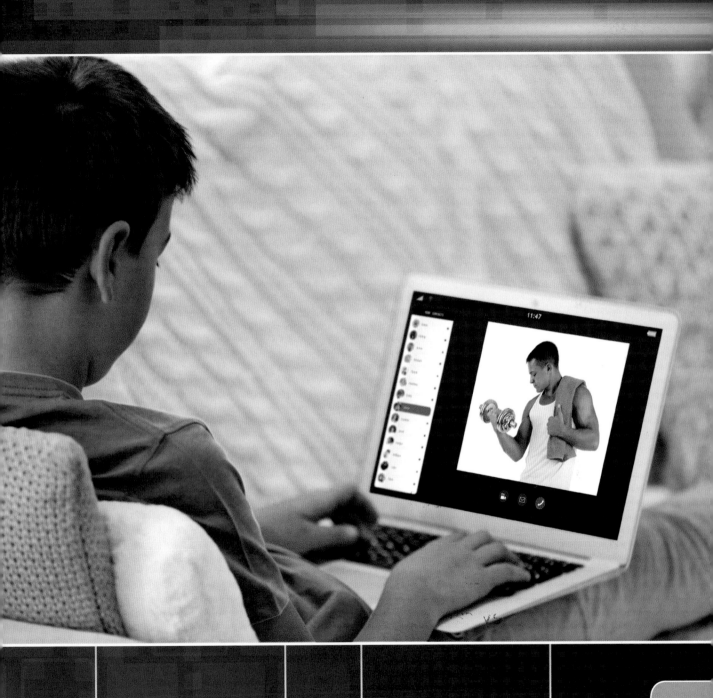

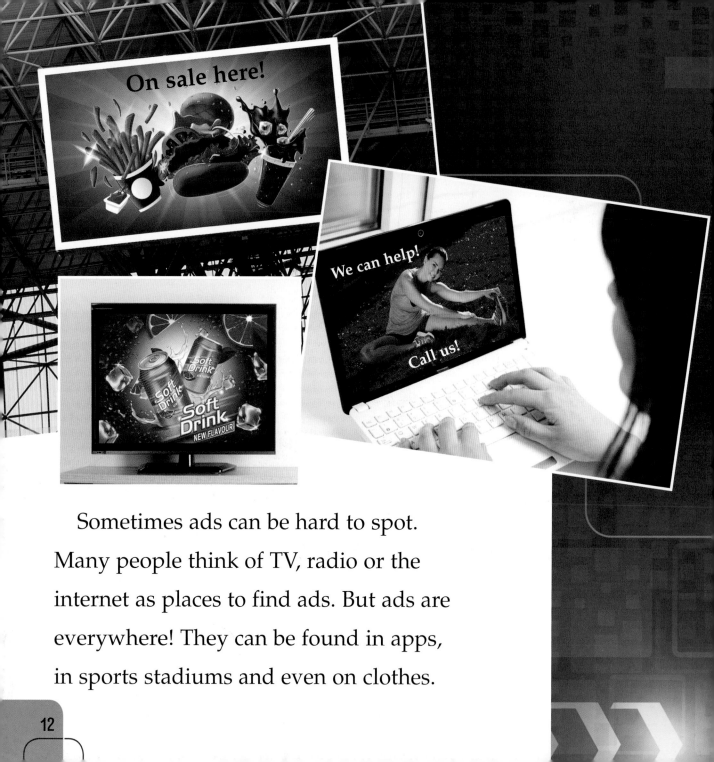

Sometimes ads can be hard to spot. Many people think of TV, radio or the internet as places to find ads. But ads are everywhere! They can be found in apps, in sports stadiums and even on clothes.

Think about it!

Brands or **logos** on cars, clothing or buildings are all advertising.

logo picture or symbol that a company puts on its products

Blogs

A blog is a website people use to keep an online diary. People who write or record blogs are called bloggers. Anyone can be a blogger. Some bloggers share real news events. Others share their thoughts and opinions about news events, games, toys or other topics. You must check other sources before trusting that information on a blog is true.

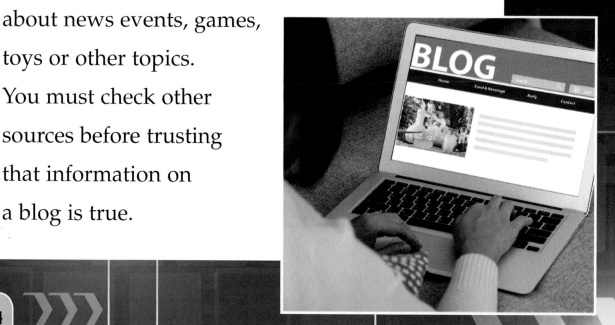

Think about it!

Blog is short for weblog. Blogs can be fun to read or watch. But make sure you pay attention and think carefully about the information a blogger is sharing. Where is the information coming from? Is it fact or opinion?

News reports

News reports give the facts about events in your local area, country and the world. A reporter's job is to provide a true account of news events. The reporter does this by answering six main questions – who, what, why, where, when and how.

You need to think carefully about news reports you read or hear. Sometimes stories that appear to be news reports are really ads. Sometimes news reports won't include all the facts or both sides of a story. Ask yourself whether or not the news report left out information. Did the report only tell one side of the story? Did the news report include the writer's opinions?

FACT Today many people read news reports they see posted on **social media**.

social media websites that allow people to share words, pictures and videos with other people

Everything in between

You see and use media every day. People share opinions with friends on social media. People visit websites to watch videos. Media messages are everywhere. Sometimes it can be hard to tell the difference between fact, fiction and opinion. TV programmes and games can be entertaining and have ads. It's easy for bloggers to mix facts and opinions. That's why it's important for you to question what you read, hear or see in the media.

TRY IT! Look at some ads in magazines or online. Imagine something you'd like to sell, such as a new toy. Write an ad for it. Who is your audience? How will you get your audience to pay attention? Will you use pictures? If you video your ad, will you use music?

Glossary

advertisement notice that calls attention to a product or an event

app programme that is downloaded to computers and mobile devices; app is short for application

audience people who hear, read or see a message

blog diary on the internet; blog is short for weblog

evidence information, items and facts that help prove something to be true or false

logo picture or symbol that a company puts on its products

persuade change a person's mind

purpose reason for which something is made or done

social media websites that allow people to share words, pictures and videos with other people

Books

I Can Write Reports (I Can Write), Anita Ganeri (Raintree, 2013)

Learning About Plagiarism (Media Literacy for Kids), Nikki Bruno Clapper (Raintree, 2015)

Let's Think About the Internet and Social Media (Let's Think About), Alex Woolf (Raintree, 2015)

Websites

www.bbc.co.uk/newsround
The BBC newsround website is just one place to stay up-to-date with news events from around the world.

www.dkfindout.com/uk/explore/top-internet-tips-to-stay-safe-online/
Looking at online media can be fun and informative – but make sure you follow these top tips to stay safe.

Comprehension questions

1. What is the purpose of a news report?

2. If you had your own blog, what would you write about and why?

3. Describe the difference between a fact and an opinion.

Index

fy nodiadau **ad⏻lygu**

CBAC TGAU

Bwyd a Maeth

Helen Buckland

HODDER
EDUCATION
AN HACHETTE UK COMPANY

CBAC TGAU Bwyd a Maeth: fy nodiadau adolygu

Addasiad Cymraeg o *WJEC GCSE Food and Nutrition (Wales): my revision notes* a gyhoeddwyd yn 2016 gan Hodder Education

Ariennir yn Rhannol gan **Lywodraeth Cymru**

Part Funded by **Welsh Government**

Cyhoeddwyd dan nawdd Cynllun Adnoddau Addysgu a Dysgu CBAC

Hoffai'r Cyhoeddwyr ddiolch i'r canlynol am roi caniatâd i atgynhyrchu deunydd hawlfraint.

Cydnabyddiaeth ffotograffau

t.7 © 1997 C Squared Studios/Photodisc/Getty Images/Eat, Drink, Dine 48; **t.9** © Imagestate Media (John Foxx)/Animals, Nature & Scenics Vol 30; **t.10** © Ingram Publishing Limited/Ingram Image Library 500-Food; **t.11** © Photodisc/Getty Images/World Commerce & Travel 5; **t.12** © Kevin Britland/Alamy Stock Photo; **t.13** © yellowj – Fotolia; **t.15** © HABAKUKKOLO – iStockphoto via Thinkstock/Getty Images; **t.16** © FOOD-pictures – Fotolia; **t.17** © Clynt Garnham Food & Drink/Alamy Stock Photo; **t.18** © BrandX/ Getty Images/Food and Textures CD X025; **t.20** © WavebreakmediaMicro – Fotolia; **t.21** © giovanni1232 – iStockphoto via Thinkstock/Getty Images; **t.22** © Photolibrary.com; © Vikram Raghuvanshi/iStockphoto.com; **t.24** © Dušan Zidar – Fotolia; © Monkey Business – Fotolia; **t.29** © matka_Wariatka – Fotolia; **t.32** © Fuse – iStockphoto via Thinkstock/Getty Images; **t.36** © Okea – Fotolia; **t.37** © Maridav – Fotolia; **t.39** © alinamd – Fotolia; **t.41** © Monkey Business – Fotolia; **t.44** © Michael Neelon(misc)/ Alamy Stock Photo; **t.47** © mezzotint_fotolia – Fotolia; **t.50** © Ross Land – Getty Images; **t.53** © BlueOrange Studio – Fotolia; **t.54** © MELBA PHOTO AGENCY/Alamy/Ingredients CD0163D; **t.55** © Awe Inspiring Images – Fotolia; © Paul_Brighton – iStockphoto via Thinkstock/ Getty Images; © Tatiana Volgutova – iStockphoto via Thinkstock/Getty Images; © Billy_Fam – iStockphoto via Thinkstock/ Getty Images; **t.56** © KucherAV – iStockphoto via Thinkstock/Getty Images; **t.58** © LOU63 – iStockphoto via Thinkstock/Getty Images; **t.59** © Hodder Education; **t.62** © marilyn barbone – Fotolia; **t.67** © Zoltan Fabian – Shutterstock; © Antonsov85 – Shutterstock; **t.68** © Kondor83 – iStockphoto via Thinkstock/Getty Images; **t.69** © F1online digitale Bildagentur GmbH/Alamy Stock Photo; **t.70** © Cultura RM/Alamy Stock Photo; **t.72** © geoffbooth19 – Fotolia; **t.73** © Gannet77 – iStockphoto via Thinkstock/Getty Images; © Stockbyte/ Photolibrary Group Ltd/Environmental Issues DV 48; **t.75** © Getty Images/Image Source – OurThreatened Environment IS236; **t.81** © Joe Gough – Fotolia; **t.82** © Mat Hayward – Shutterstock; © M.studio – Fotolia; **t.85** © Ryan McVay – iStockphoto via Thinkstock/Getty Images; **t.93** © funkyfood London – Paul Williams/ Alamy Stock Photo; **t.94** © MediablitzImages – Fotolia; **t.95** © Monkey Business – Fotolia; **t.101** © Ingram Publishing – iStockphoto via Thinkstock/Getty Images; © Thomas Northcut – iStockphoto via Thinkstock/ Getty Images; **t.102** © Oleg Pchelov – Shutterstock; © Ciaran Walsh/iStockphoto.com; **t.103** © Andrew Callaghan/Hodder Education; **t.104** © Ian O'Leary/Getty Images; **t.105** © Serghei Starus – iStockphoto via Thinkstock/Getty Images; © Penny Burt – iStockphoto via Thinkstock/Getty Images; © Lee Lian Chong – iStockphoto via Thinkstock/Getty Images; © Uncle_ Bob - iStockphoto via Thinkstock/Getty Images; © zhaubasar – iStockphoto via Thinkstock/Getty Images; **t.107** © Doug Steley A/Alamy Stock Photo; **t.109** © Alex Segre/Alamy Stock Photo; **t.110** © ranplett/iStockphoto; **t.111** © HLPhoto – Fotolia; **t.113** © moreimages – Shutterstock

Cydnabyddiaeth

Gwnaed pob ymdrech i gysylltu â'r holl ddeiliaid hawlfraint, ond os oes unrhyw rai wedi'u hesgeuluso'n anfwriadol, bydd y cyhoeddwyr yn falch o wneud y trefniadau angenrheidiol ar y cyfle cyntaf.

Er y gwnaed pob ymdrech i sicrhau bod cyfeiriadau gwefannau yn gywir adeg mynd i'r wasg, nid yw Hodder Education yn gyfrifol am gynnwys unrhyw wefan y cyfeirir ati yn y llyfr hwn. Weithiau mae'n bosibl dod o hyd i dudalen we a adleolwyd trwy deipio cyfeiriad tudalen gartref gwefan yn ffenestr LlAU (*URL*) eich porwr.

Polisi Hachette UK yw defnyddio papurau sy'n gynhyrchion naturiol, adnewyddadwy ac ailgylchadwy o goed a dyfwyd mewn coedwigoedd cynaliadwy. Disgwylir i'r prosesau torri coed a gweithgynhyrchu gydymffurfio â rheoliadau amgylcheddol y wlad y mae'r cynnyrch yn tarddu ohoni.

Archebion

Bookpoint Ltd, 130 Park Drive, Milton Park, Abingdon, Oxon OX14 4SE
ffôn: (44) 01235 827720
ffacs: (44) 01235 400454
e-bost: education@bookpoint.co.uk
Mae'r llinellau ar agor rhwng 9.00 a 17.00 o ddydd Llun i ddydd Sadwrn, gyda gwasanaeth ateb negeseuon 24 awr. Gallwch hefyd archebu trwy ein gwefan: www.hoddereducation.co.uk.

ISBN 978 1 5104 2708 2

© Helen Buckland 2016 (yr argraffiad Saesneg)

Cyhoeddwyd gyntaf yn 2016 gan

Hodder Education,
an Hachette UK Company,
Carmelite House,
50 Victoria Embankment
London EC4Y 0DZ
www.hoddereducation.co.uk

© CBAC 2019 (yr argraffiad Cymraeg hwn ar gyfer CBAC)

Llun y clawr © MELBA PHOTO AGENCY/Alamy/Ingredients CD0163D.

Darluniau gan Aptara Inc.

Teiposodwyd yn Bembo Std Regular 11/13 pts gan Aptara Inc.

Argraffwyd yn Sbaen.

Mae cofnod catalog y teitl hwn ar gael gan y Llyfrgell Brydeinig.